A Rug and a Bag

By RL Lane

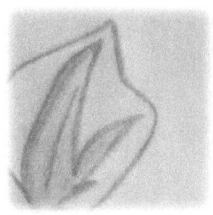

Illustrations by RL Lane

Cover Design by RL Lane

"The rug was rolled under one arm and the bag was slung over my shoulder. I walked on the path through the woods with my wares. I saw him up ahead with his dog. I didn't want to scare him. There was no one else around. I finally caught up with him. He stopped and turned around and asked me where I was going with all that stuff. I didn't answer. I just told him how beautiful his dog was. Gavin. Or maybe it's Gaven. Either way, he was beautiful. Running ahead looking around to see what else was in those woods…" RL Lane

We chatted as we walked through the woods. I didn't tell him the real reason I was walking with all that stuff. He probably knew there was more to the story. He said he didn't think I was the bag lady blowing through the woods. He seemed like a wise man…one who could probably offer a lot of good advice…

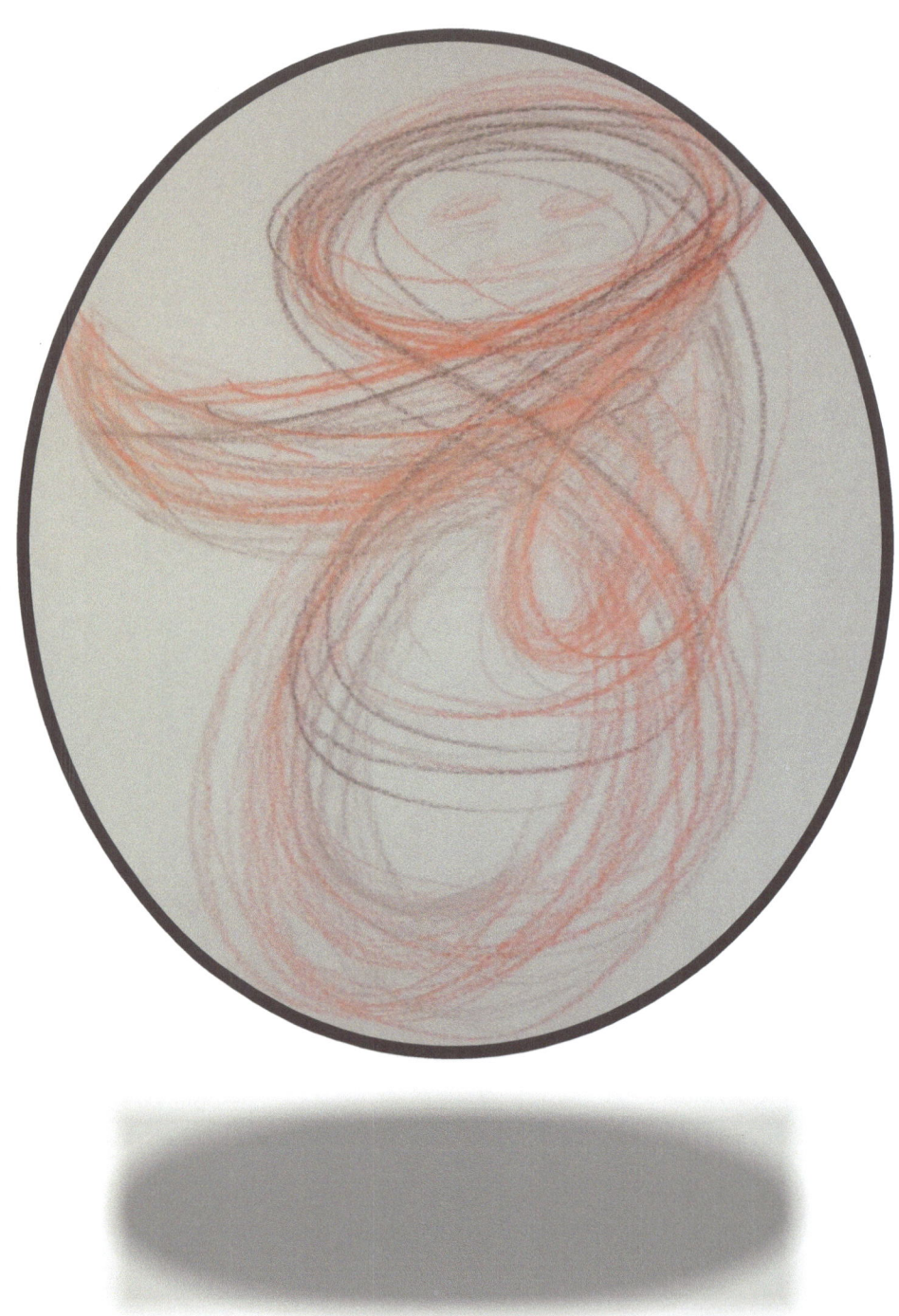

I am thankful he wasn't mean. Someone who would have ignored me or looked at me with disgust. Stay away some would say. It's hard for a lot of people to see beyond the outer layer. Some never bother to look. Oh. What treasure they have missed…

Any person met along the way…any conversation has the potential to be a gem…

Not the gem in the shiny ring

Not the ring the boxers dance around

Not the dance the people step to

Not the step down to the fires

Not the fires of eternal flames

Not the flames of everlasting light

Oh yes.

The flames of everlasting light…

The woods are in the same small NJ town as the other woods I wrote about in "The Walk of a Thousand Moods". There were a lot less moods on this trip. I wanted this book to be happy. The man I met seemed like a happy person. His dog was certainly happy. I picked some of my favorite drawings for the pages of his book…

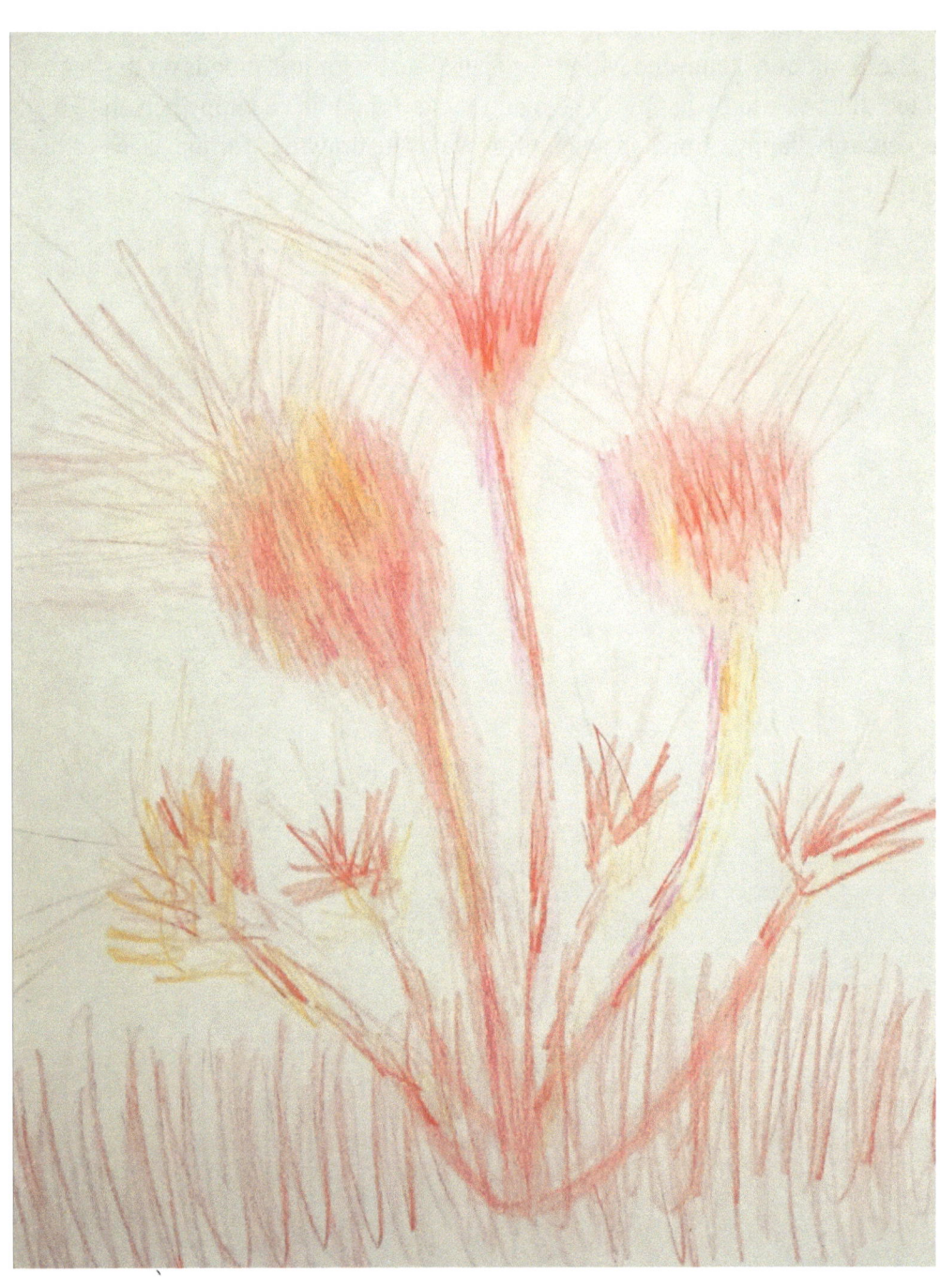

"Field of Fireworks"

"Dandelion Puffs"

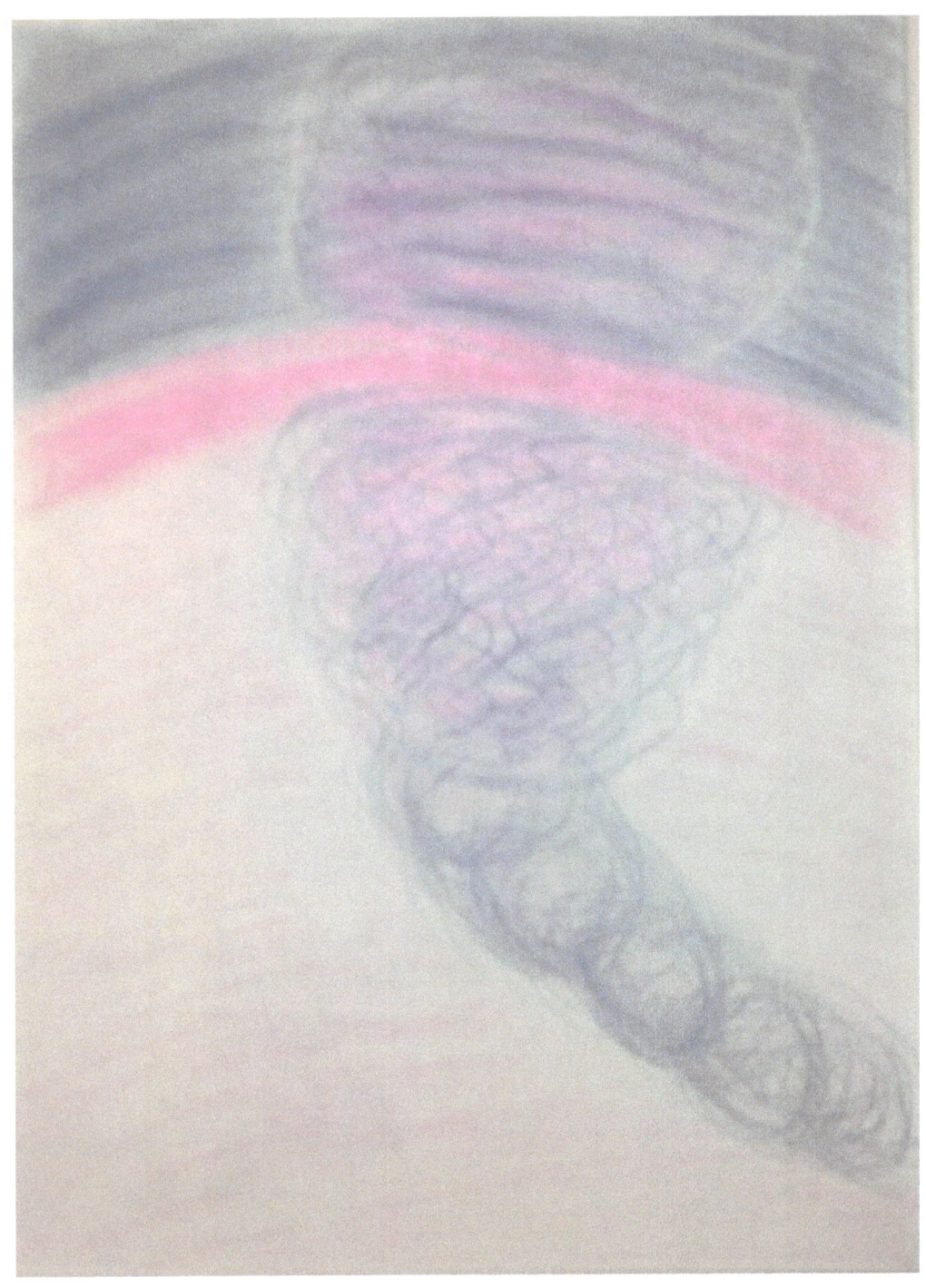

"Break the storm…so you can see the rainbow"

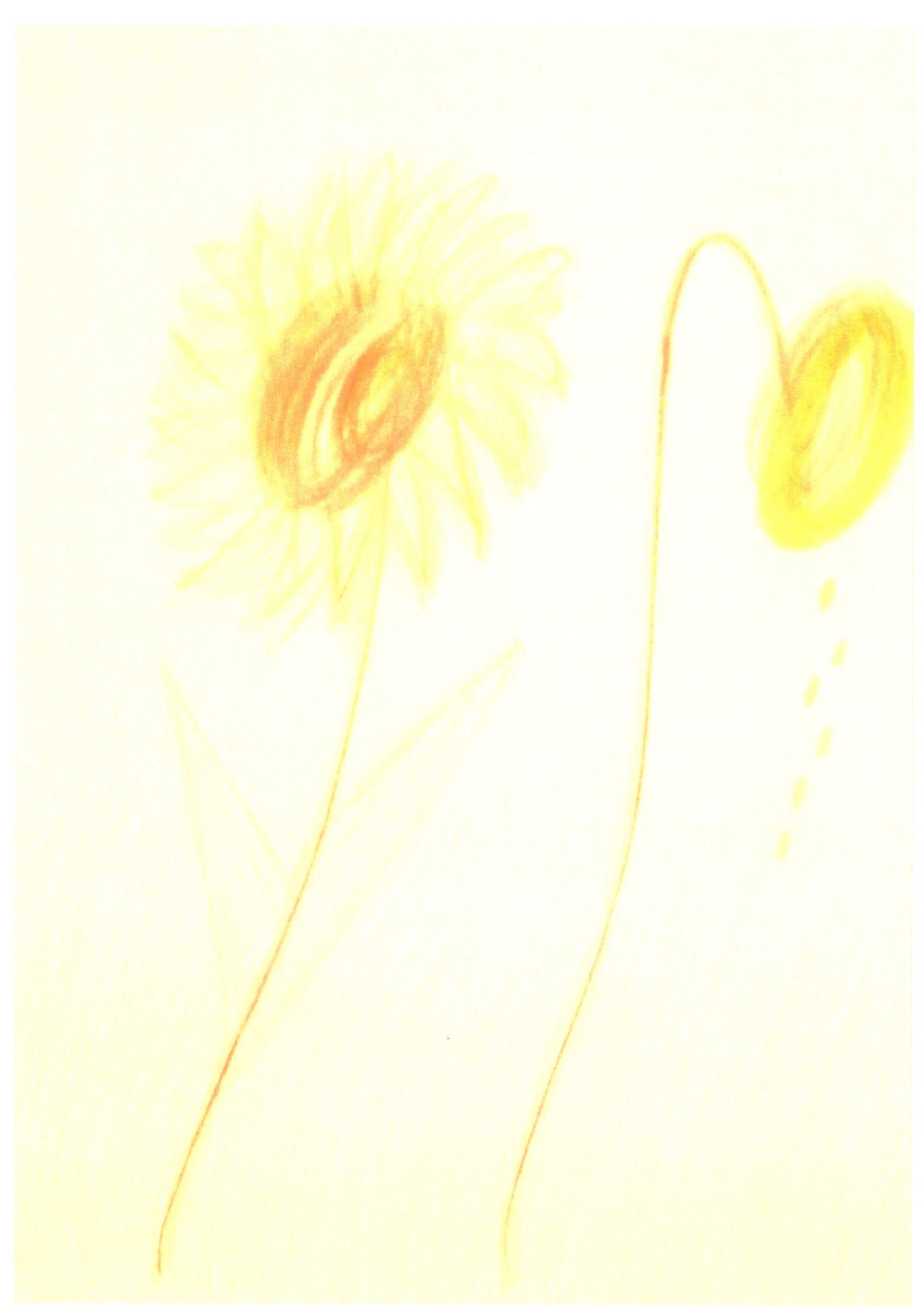

"I'll help you…"

He made a difference to me. He made that trip through the woods seem shorter. I stopped several times on the benches to rest along the way. I was just glad it wasn't raining that day in the woods…

The benches along the way have been dedicated to loved ones who have already been lost. I wonder if there are ones to represent the loved ones lost to drugs and alcohol. Maybe that could be RL Lane's bench someday…

"Dedicated to the loved ones who lost the drug and alcohol battle…what a valiant battle we did fight." I'm sure everyone knows of at least one person…

I really did want his book to be happy. Why is it so sad? Maybe it isn't so sad. Maybe it is only sad if battles are lost without a valiant effort. If we don our armor and pull out the sword…fight bravely to the end…are we still a knight of honor if we do not slay the dragon?

I didn't fight very hard the first half of my life. You can't have a battle if there is no one willing to fight. I am glad I learned how to fight now…the second half will be a battle…

Who will be the opposing force?

Will the forces be from the beyond?

Where will the encounter take place?

Who will be the "winner"?

About the Author and Illustrator

RL Lane has published the EcarreT series and a collection of short stories featuring the illustrations, along with the children's books "G" and "How to Catch a Goast". The series begins with "Chapel Street Signs"…

…unexplained connections that challenge us to beli ve. A woman, a Dad a Doctor, a cat and mouse, a horse and tale tell their stories. "Do you beli ve in spirits?" I asked my friend. "Well look", he said, "I believe there are things that cannot be explained…" Oh. Plus, hear ov a Mom's battle with her struggle to connect to the woman…her little girl.

Welcome to EcarreT…a world
Where everyone cares
Why did I have to create it in…

A fiction fantasy world?

You may already know why, but you will see regardless of what you believe as a girl's journey of love and faith on her "Touring Machine" take her on the best journey of her mundane life. A life well on its way takes a turn in a direction that could've never been seen or even dreamed…

The author can be contacted at:

RosaLeeeLane@gmail.com
www.Amazon.com/author/readrllane

Twitter.com/readrllane

Books by RL Lane

EcarreT Series:

Chapel Street Signs

secret Life OV an antE

Sri Town

Which of EcarreT

Hand of Heven

Short Stories:

Mon Treal, The Odd Cod, The Half Day, No Gift for Greed, Aunt Elm & Uncle Poc, What Would Caitlin Wear, The Bag of Scribbles, Mr. Uraly's Italy, A not G, Johnni and Georg, A Cup of Butter, The Walk of a THOUSAND Moods, Storm Window, The Rugs, Cones of Ice Crème, Angel-A, The Art of Sri Town, Under Water, The Dinner Party, The Vault, No Lines to Erase, Rock of Snow, Polka Dot Rain Boots

Children's:

G

How to Catch a Goast

Battle – An encounter between opposing forces…